Evening All Afternoon

Anna Ziegler

methuen | drama
LONDON • NEW YORK • OXFORD • NEW DELHI • SYDNEY

METHUEN DRAMA

Bloomsbury Publishing Plc, 50 Bedford Square, London, WC1B 3DP, UK
Bloomsbury Publishing Inc, 1359 Broadway, New York, NY 10018, USA
Bloomsbury Publishing Ireland, 29 Earlsfort Terrace, Dublin 2, D02 AY28, Ireland

BLOOMSBURY, METHUEN DRAMA and the Methuen
Drama logo are trademarks of Bloomsbury Publishing Plc

First published in Great Britain 2026

Copyright © Anna Ziegler, 2026

Anna Ziegler has asserted her right under the Copyright, Designs
and Patents Act, 1988, to be identified as author of this work.

Front cover design and illustration by Megan Wilson
Back cover photography by Helen Murray

All rights reserved. No part of this publication may be: i) reproduced or transmitted in
any form, electronic or mechanical, including photocopying, recording or by means of
any information storage or retrieval system without prior permission in writing from
the publishers; or ii) used or reproduced in any way for the training, development or
operation of artificial intelligence (AI) technologies, including generative
AI technologies. The rights holders expressly reserve this publication from the
text and data mining exception as per Article 4(3) of the Digital Single
Market Directive (EU) 2019/790.

Bloomsbury Publishing Plc does not have any control over, or responsibility for,
any third-party websites referred to or in this book. All internet addresses given in
this book were correct at the time of going to press. The author and publisher regret
any inconvenience caused if addresses have changed or sites have ceased
to exist, but can accept no responsibility for any such changes.

No rights in incidental music or songs contained in the work are hereby granted
and performance rights for any performance/presentation whatsoever
must be obtained from the respective copyright owners.

All rights whatsoever in this play are strictly reserved and application for performance
etc. should be made before rehearsals to Creative Artists Agency,
405 Lexington Avenue, 22nd Floor, New York, NY 10174, USA.
No performance may be given unless a licence has been obtained

A catalogue record for this book is available from the British Library.

A catalog record for this book is available from the Library of Congress.

ISBN: PB: 978-1-3506-1876-3
ePDF: 978-1-3506-1877-0
eBook: 978-1-3506-1878-7

Series: Modern Plays

Typeset by Westchester Publishing Services
Printed and bound in Great Britain

For product safety related questions contact productsafety@bloomsbury.com.

To find out more about our authors and books visit
www.bloomsbury.com and sign up for our newsletters.

Evening All Afternoon

Anna Ziegler

Evening All Afternoon had its world premiere at the Donmar Warehouse on 14 February 2026 with the following cast and creative team:

Jennifer	**Anastasia Hille**
Delilah	**Erin Kellyman**
Director	**Diyan Zora**
Designer	**Basia Bińkowska**
Lighting Designer	**Natasha Chivers**
Composer & Sound Designer	**Adam Cork**
Associate Director	**Lucy Jane Atkinson**
Casting Director	**Lotte Hines CDG**
Dialect Coach	**Aundrea Fudge**
Voice Coach	**Barbara Houseman**
Movement Director	**Sara Green**
Production Manager	**Simon MacColl**
Company Stage Manager	**Cheryl Firth**
Deputy Stage Manager	**Shakira Taylor-Knight**
Assistant Stage Manager	**Qian Yan Tan**
Costume Supervisor	**Rosy Emmerich**
Props Supervisor	**Katie Balmorth**
Assistant Set & Costume Designer	**Mana Sadri Irani**
Assistant Lighting Designer	**Amelia Hawkes**
Stage Management Intern	**Lee Robinson**

"I mean what a thing, to have a mother."

To mine.

Evening All Afternoon

Anna Ziegler

I would give you some violets, but
they withered all when my father
died.
     —Shakespeare, *Hamlet*

"It was evening all afternoon.
It was snowing
And it was going to snow.
The blackbird sat
In the cedar-limbs".
 —Wallace Stevens, "Thirteen Ways
    of Looking at a Blackbird"

Characters

Jennifer—A British woman in her late fifties or early sixties. Curious, self-effacing, and observant.
Delilah—An American woman in her early twenties. Sharp, wry, and emotionally raw.

The final script used during performances may differ to the version in this playtext due to changes made in rehearsals and previews.

Jennifer *faces the audience. On the other side of the stage is the bar of a fancy London restaurant. (It need not be literal in any way.)*
Jennifer *is neat and tidy but a bit old-fashioned. She seems older than she is, given the way she dresses and carries herself. She's quite proper (but not posh).*
Delilah *(not yet on stage) is a college student, American, and not remotely proper.*
It's January 2020.

JENNIFER
(to the audience, conversational)
Of course we didn't plan it this way.
Getting married.
What's the saying?
"Life is what happens when you're busy making other plans."
Now who said that?
(She shrugs)
The thing about getting to be this age is that when you reach for things
you often discover they're no longer there:
words, the title of that book you read, oh—last week probably,
people's names of course, the cup of tea
you're sure you left right there.
Also, of course, the wear and tear in the limbs, in the joints.
You bend down to pick something up—let's say that *all-important* mobile
(why are all important things in life so incredibly slippery?)
and there it is: you put your back out.
It was actually in this way that I met John. Flat on my back and entirely helpless.

DELILAH
(entering, to the audience)
I was like you've got to be kidding me. Like, is that a joke? . . . Step class?? But *no*, she doubled down. She was like:

JENNIFER
(*moving over with* **Delilah** *to stand at the counter of the bar*)
Of course I'm serious. I always so enjoyed
step aerobics.
My friend Sarah and I used to go together—and I don't
think I've ever been in better shape. It's really quite
invigorating. I'm not sure why I stopped.

DELILAH
(*to the audience, with an eye roll*)
And then she like, looks down.

JENNIFER
(*sadly*)
Oh no, I remember why I stopped.

DELILAH
(*to the audience*)
Seriously?
It can't seriously be my job right now to ask some
kind of follow-up question after she's just—apparently
in all sincerity—proposed that given she's about
to be my stepmother (which *I* know but she doesn't
know I know) we should sign up together to do a
step class?
Like, this is for real?

JENNIFER
I'm sorry. I just got a little. I'm sorry.

DELILAH
What are you sorry about?

JENNIFER
Well, I don't think I should impose any of my . . .

DELILAH
Feelings?

JENNIFER
Right. Those. On you.

DELILAH
I thought you didn't have those. That British people are just kind of repressed.

JENNIFER
Oh, we are.

(*An uncomfortable silence*)

JENNIFER
(*looking at her watch*)
Gosh, I hope they don't cancel our reservation. I booked this two months ago.

(*Again,* **Delilah** *doesn't say anything*)

It's meant to be quite good. And you can't get in unless you book in advance, so I did.

DELILAH
Well, that was very forward-thinking of you, Jennifer.

JENNIFER
Was that, um.

DELILAH
What?

JENNIFER
Nothing. I just thought it might've been a touch of what my mother would've called . . . cheek.

DELILAH
Cheek?

JENNIFER
Oh, it means, um—

DELILAH
I know what cheek means.

JENNIFER
Right. So then was it?

DELILAH
I don't think so. But it doesn't matter.

JENNIFER
Doesn't it?

DELILAH
I couldn't control how you saw me if I tried.

JENNIFER
(*as in, you could be a lot less surly*)
Oh I think you could.

DELILAH
If you say so.

JENNIFER
Listen. This is supposed to be nice. We have something to share with you. Something important. Nice and important. Not something scary. Nothing like that.

DELILAH
(*to the audience*)
Like I said, I know that they're going to tell me they're getting married. I know because my dad can't keep a secret to save his life and spilled the beans, over breakfast on Sunday, while *literally* spilling beans all down his shirt. All I could do was laugh and then Dad said "Delilah, this is serious" and I was like, "I know it is, but if I take it seriously I'll get very upset and also please for godsake change your shirt, you look like you threw up."

JENNIFER
Did you hear me, Delilah?

DELILAH
I heard you. And, like . . . that's fine. Get married.

JENNIFER
What? I didn't say that we were—

DELILAH
I know.

JENNIFER
Oh. Did he . . . ?

DELILAH
Yeah, Dad doesn't keep anything from me. We're kinda like this—

(*She crosses her fingers to indicate how tight they are.*)

JENNIFER
Ah. And did he, um. When he told you, did he sound . . . would you say he sounded pleased?

DELILAH
I don't know.
But, like, he wouldn't have. He wouldn't have sounded pleased when he told me because he knows *I* wouldn't be pleased. To get that news. Because of my mom and all.

JENNIFER
Right. Of course. Even a number of years later those things can still feel quite fresh.

DELILAH
They really can, Jennifer.

JENNIFER
My own mother died not too—

DELILAH
So how come you never got married before?

JENNIFER
Oh, I don't know . . . I guess life just . . . took me in a different direction.

DELILAH
What does that mean?

JENNIFER
Just that, well, hm. I mean, I suppose I got very invested in my work—

DELILAH
Which is . . . organizing medical records?

JENNIFER
Well, we do more than organize them. We keep them up to date. We store them.

DELILAH
Okay.

JENNIFER
It might not be electrifying, or what do you young people say? It doesn't shake the earth, or—

DELILAH
Do young people say that?

JENNIFER
And of course I had my mother to care for. She had a number of . . . health issues

that all seemed to require a lot of time . . . on my part. Not that I begrudged her in any way.

DELILAH
But you still had time to like picket outside abortion clinics and stuff.

JENNIFER
Sorry?

DELILAH
Dad said you're, like, pro-life or something.

JENNIFER
I've never protested outside an abortion clinic. Or anywhere else for that matter.

DELILAH
Okay so you have beliefs but you don't feel super strongly about them. Not enough to *do* anything about them.

JENNIFER
You know, I don't know if we should . . .

DELILAH
What?

(*Beat.* **Jennifer** *decides whether or not to pursue the topic.*)

JENNIFER
The thing is, *my mother* felt quite strongly. About the delicacy and miraculous-ness of life. That it ought to be handled with care. She used to volunteer in maternity wards, when she was young, to help the new mothers. Maybe an excuse to hold the babies. She liked the way their heads smelled.

DELILAH
I like babies too but I don't think any woman should be forced to have one if she doesn't want to. Or isn't ready.

JENNIFER
(*a little too conspicuously changing the subject*)
So what are you studying these days exactly?

DELILAH
You know I'm getting a degree in history, right?

JENNIFER
I did know that.

DELILAH
So, yeah: history. That's what I'm studying.

JENNIFER
The thing is, though . . . history is rather *large*.

DELILAH
In some senses.

JENNIFER
In what sense is it *not* very large?

DELILAH
In the same way that your life is both very large and also infinitesimally small. Everything's relative.

JENNIFER
Well, yes.

DELILAH
But if you want specifics, then specifically I've found the one professor with whom I can study the role of Black Americans during the period of Reconstruction after the Civil War and the way regular people who did heroic things are depicted in art.

JENNIFER
What kind of art?

DELILAH
That's your next question?

JENNIFER
I didn't realize there were right and wrong questions—

DELILAH
Like, paintings, drawings, stories. You know: art.

JENNIFER
And how are they depicted? The regular people.

DELILAH
Insufficiently.

JENNIFER
Oh yes?

DELILAH
And as a result there's like almost no one to relate to. Which makes it hard to understand what they were going through.

JENNIFER
Do you need to relate to someone to understand what they're going through?

DELILAH
I think so, yeah.

JENNIFER
Then if only we could bring the dead back to life. To explain themselves to us.

DELILAH
(*quietly*)
Yeah, exactly.

JENNIFER
Also, I can relate. To the idea of looking for people to relate to. I've never been big on . . . people, really.

DELILAH
You don't like people?

JENNIFER
That's not quite what I meant.

DELILAH
I mean, it's okay. I don't like people either.

JENNIFER
Don't you?

DELILAH
Not if I can help it.

JENNIFER
The thing is I'm not sure if I dislike people or just dislike that they seem to dislike me.

(*Awkward beat.*)

DELILAH
(*this has gotten too intimate*)
God, where is my dad?

JENNIFER
He really is so often late.

DELILAH
That's what happens when you won't wear a watch. Or keep your phone on.

JENNIFER
It *is* one of his odd quirks.

DELILAH
He thinks we're not really living if we're constantly checking the time. Why walk around with the hourglass of your own life emptying out right there on your wrist.

JENNIFER
I think it's more about staying in the moment.

DELILAH
I would want to think that too if I was about to marry him.
But don't be fooled. He's a weird guy.
. . . and it got worse, when my mother died. After that
he would only wear a watch at work. Time didn't make
sense to him anymore probably because life didn't
make sense.
He really loved her, you know.

JENNIFER
I know that.

DELILAH
But I'm sure he loves you too. That said, when he met up
with my mom, he was always on time.

(*And then* **Delilah** *is gone.*)

JENNIFER
(*to the audience*)
Right.
You reach for something and then it isn't there at all.
Or what's there isn't at all what you expected.
For instance, I never expected to get married.
And if I did—have that somewhere in the back of my mind—
I didn't think it would be like *this*.
I didn't think I'd be this old or that my husband would be
slightly . . . less old or that he would have a child who, as the
clichés go, wants nothing to do with me.
I'm really not that bad, after all.
I try hard. Which John says might be the problem.
I'm reminded of a strange outing with my mother near the
end of her life.
I was at work when she called. "Jennifer, there's a *magician*
on in the West End!"

I was eating toast at my desk; sometimes I'd play a game
with myself involving
not making a single crumb. Usually I failed.
I had lived my entire life alone.
Well, in the sense of a romantic partner.
Of course there were a few, but nothing that stuck,
no one who glued himself in some irrevocable way to
my soul.
I did spend a good deal of time with my mother.
Who was also alone.
And I'd like to say that when we were together we were no
longer alone
but really we were alone together, which was still better than
the alternative.
So when she said "there's a magician on in the West End!"
I had to book the tickets. Right away.
The next evening I called her a taxi
because she didn't like to use her walking frame;
she thought it made her look old and I didn't have the heart
to say no, everything *else* is what makes you look old.
We had very good seats. The show begins
and out walks a man in a very neat suit;
he starts doing his sleight of hand tricks, his card tricks;
a bag from Tescos that looks to be holding
something heavy
turns out to be entirely empty.
It's all just . . . fine.
But *then* you realize he's underperforming;
this is the *setup* of the show—so that when he does,
finally, disappear, it's really something—you don't know
how he does it; it's stunning, actually, his absence.

How that can just happen to a person.

I look over at my mother and she's circling
an ad in the program for a discount at a nearby restaurant.
Afterwards, she says, "I was so bored, Jennifer.
To me there is nothing interesting

about things disappearing; things disappear from my life all
the time.
People disappear all the time.
In retrospect one really shouldn't take an old person to a
magic show."

You see, she was full of complaints,
and mostly I understood them.
It must be so hard to be that age. Still I sometimes
wondered if an occasional thank you
might be in order—I did try hard to make her happy—
only to banish the thought;
I shouldn't need gratitude for doing right
by this person to whom I owed a great deal
and who, remember, Jennifer, won't be here forever.

And she wasn't.
Not two months later I'd find
myself in her empty flat, trying to
sort through the mess. And the silence,
where once there was so much idle chatter.
Meaningless and yet it filled the space.
Filled my life, really. Gave it shape.
How could I possibly think I could be here without her?
And then my back went—and the pain was . . .
And this wasn't the first time in my life
when I felt I might die, but then, as now,
I wasn't ready and so finally I shouted at the top of my lungs
Help me!
. . . and someone actually heard me all the way
across the hall, in his flat; someone heard me,
and he came rushing inside
and that was John
and he scooped me up in more ways than one.

DELILAH
It's all bullshit.
It just sounds nice,

because of the accent.
That's what my mother would say
about *(in an over-the-top accent)* "Englishmen."
Of which my dad was one.
Unlike her—she was Jamaican with the most
beautiful accent in the world
and everyone said I had her eyes and my father's smile
but really I didn't look a thing like either one of them;
for a while I secretly assumed I was adopted and was
actually happy about it,
happy that I was a mystery and not just this jigsaw puzzle
where the pieces didn't quite fit.

And oh my god she *never* wanted to move here. England?
Never!
My mom was like: England is an old country for old people.
I guarantee she'd be doing backflips in her grave
if she knew
that after she died, my dad high-tailed it back here from
Brooklyn
and dragged me right along with him.

JENNIFER
Was it love at first sight? People like to ask that question.
And I mean, maybe it was.
It was definitely something at first sight.

DELILAH
Not that I want to talk about my mother.
I don't talk about her. Or think about her;
not because I didn't like her but because
I liked her so much.

JENNIFER
Maybe it was relief.
As though this idea you didn't realize you
were waiting to understand has now crystallized
and stands before you,

sagging pants and all.
One of the first things I'll do, I thought,
when we're married, is nip to Marks and Spencer
and buy him new underwear.
And it's in that moment you realize you will—
or want to be, a wife. Reminded a little
of that moment when you finished
your last exam at uni and it hit you:
you won't ever have to take another one.

DELILAH
I saw Jennifer before she saw me.
In that I spied on her.
Oh yeah. I spied the *shit* out of her.
I saw how she'd take her comb out of her purse
when he left the room
and run it quickly through her hair.
I don't think I knew what powdered your nose
really meant until Jennifer.
I mean, she would literally put powder on her nose.
It was like she was born in another time.
And I guess she was.
Seven years older than my dad.
Whereas my mother was ten years younger.
As though my dad felt it was only right, this time,
to marry a ghost—

JENNIFER
It was a lovely courtship.
Once I could walk again of course.
Not that I had very much to compare it to
but it certainly compared favorably
to being alone and while I missed
my mother terribly, it also compared favorably
to my evenings with her because there's something
strange, or at least there was for us,
about being two women on a sofa
with nowhere to go.

DELILAH
Also she's SO conservative.
Or maybe she's not but she did feel "quite sorry
for Theresa May"
which, sure, but to me that's like my friend Tracy going to
subpar K-pop concerts because she feels bad for the bands.
Not that Jennifer's political. "Not a political animal,"
my dad says, so who cares. But, like . . . I do.

JENNIFER
And oh my god I'd never eaten so much! If I was the type
to gain weight, I'd've put on half a stone!
I mean: Thai, Japanese, *Ethiopian*! We went
to all sorts, and we talked about everything—
oh, everything—the world, what was in it, what we liked
and didn't like, our differences, which were
numerous, perhaps unquantifiable; all of it—except
I now realize, what it was he liked about *me* . . .

DELILAH
I care that what she believes is rooted in a system
that basically subjugates people who look like me,
so, like, I have to assume she's at least a little bit racist,
right?
I mean, you can't really just be a fiscal conservative.
And why my dad doesn't give a shit is beyond me;
he's as liberal as they come, or, like . . . maybe he's not;
maybe he got near fifty and it was like, poof:
now you're gonna read *The Sunday Times* instead of
The Observer and start talking about "the market"
during dinner. Also Jennifer
never wears a shirt untucked.
So, like, yeah.
She's conservative.

JENNIFER
She was obviously a very clever girl.
And obviously not at all enamored of me.

Which hurt a bit more coming from someone
who clearly discerned the world with a certain
degree of acuity. I mean, really, what was
so unlikeable about me? If anything, I am
too agreeable; if anything I stay out of people's way
more than I should. I mean, of course I have
my own ideas. But I don't feel I should impose
them on anyone. I suppose it's how I was brought up:
don't speak about politics, or religion
or money, and absolutely do not speak of . . . well, you
know.
Which began to be problematic with John
because he wanted to talk about it all the time;
his years in America must have made him voluble
about matters of . . . For instance he wanted me
(*she whispers*)
to say what *I wanted*—in bed, I mean—which was just . . .
(*The most horrifying thing she can imagine*)
But where Delilah was concerned,
I tried to take my cues from John.
And he said of course we had to have a wedding
and of course Delilah would be involved.
"Your maid of honor!" he said,
as though he'd just discovered electricity.
And he thought it would be good if the request
came directly from me and as it happened, the next Sunday
Delilah came over for lunch, during which she complained vociferously
about my roast—to be fair, it was a bit dry—
but was it so inedible one had to eject it from one's mouth?
So, yes, after this very successful meal, I found her.

Hello Delilah, I said.

And she looked at me as though there was more I should say before she would deign to speak.

So I said:

Hello Delilah (again, like a buffoon) and then: how are you today?

DELILAH
I'm fine.

JENNIFER
Good! That's, well, that's very good.
It's something to be fine, isn't it?
We're not *always* fine, are we?

DELILAH
I'm not really fine; I was just being polite.

JENNIFER
Oh. I see.

DELILAH
You look really scared right now.

JENNIFER
I'm not at all scared. I just sense a bit of cheek coming on.

DELILAH
Is that right? More cheek?

JENNIFER
(*sharper*)
Why don't you just tell me what's troubling you?

DELILAH
Well for one thing I'm being brutally attacked from the inside. I've gone through so many tampons I might seriously be creating a supply chain issue.

JENNIFER
(*delicately*)
Oh—is this, ah, are we talking about, a, um, a matter of . . . your menses?

DELILAH
Or maybe I'm not fine because I had one of those
revelations the other day that my friends aren't actually my
friends, like maybe I don't like them, like at all, even Tracy,
and also I'm not fine because today's my mother's birthday
and no one's said a word about it, which makes me feel like
I'm on a different planet because it's *all* I can think about
and also her *last* birthday when we rented a convertible and
drove all over lower Manhattan and mom yelled *(lightly, in
her mother's voice)* "it's your birthday, bald man!" or "happy
birthday, girl in the red scarf" to random folks on the street
even though it was *her* birthday, her thirty-eighth birthday,
five fucking years ago, and then, you know, by her next
birthday she was dead.

(**Delilah** *stomps off.*)

JENNIFER
(to the audience)
So you see I didn't get the chance to ask her that day, to be
my maid of honor.
And when the wedding took place
she sat in the back in a headpiece that looked suspiciously
like a veil you'd wear at a funeral.

DELILAH
The day my father married Jennifer
I was going through some shit.
Well, that whole semester I'd been going through some shit.
And my dad didn't know about it and Tracy
didn't know about it even though I was basically
living at her place because Trevor, my roommate,
was a slob and couldn't manage
to keep his crap in his room and also did all this
baking at really odd hours.
But that wasn't the problem. The problem
had to do with a general sense of, yeah I guess
you'd call it ennui

that had started to find its way into everything,
as though everything I touched or talked about
was coated in this sticky layer of sadness or . . . insignificance.
As though I had kind of . . . lost all my mirth . . .
So you can't blame me for cutting corners *one time*
when I didn't feel like writing my weekly art history paper.
But a few days later, in Professor Greenhill's office hours,
he gives me this look, this *look* like he's just scratched off
the absolute winning fucking lottery ticket.
Delilah, he said, is it fair to assume you correctly cited all
your sources?
All innocent—but also managing somehow to touch my arm—
and before I can even respond he goes on:
"Oh and I almost forgot: last night I had a dream about
you . . .
you were an artist, and you painted a painting.
And I *bought* it." And, for some reason, I wanted to ask,
like, was it expensive? Like, how much are we talking here?
But then he went on, "it was I must say, a very pleasurable
dream."
I think at that point I knew that when I got home
there'd be an email waiting for me, which there was;
he had more to share about how I might connect two of my
ideas—
and hoped I could come in to discuss them—but not to his
office,
to his home, and when I asked why, he just emailed back
a photo of my, okay, lightly plagiarized fucking paper,
and this is why, after my dad's wedding, I found myself
crying in the bathroom because what should I do?
Drop out of intro art history, which is not only a prerequisite
for my concentration in History but, the way I see it, for my
life—
I mean, my mother was an artist and art historian
(well, a professor of folklore and ethnomusicology with a
focus on Caribbean art and ritual)
and always said art is a comfort in that it never dies
and also it teaches you what people were thinking

which is probably the hardest thing in the world, to understand what's going on in someone else's brain.

JENNIFER
(*entering*)
Oh gosh, Delilah.

DELILAH
What?

JENNIFER
You're crying.

DELILAH
No I'm not.

JENNIFER
What can I do to help?

DELILAH
(*to the audience*)
And she kneels down in her white dress on the bathroom floor and the dress gets a bit scuffed but I guess she doesn't care.

JENNIFER
Delilah?

DELILAH
There's nothing you can do.

JENNIFER
I'm so sorry—John should have seen to it that you two had some time together this morning, just the two of you.

DELILAH
Oh. Well. That's not on you.

JENNIFER
Would talking help?

DELILAH
Are you a shrink?

JENNIFER
I'm not "a shrink."

DELILAH
(*blurting out*)
Well, have you ever been in a position where you felt someone was taking advantage of you?

JENNIFER
In what way?

DELILAH
I don't know.

JENNIFER
Hm. For someone to want to take advantage of you you'd need to have something worthwhile to offer. Something someone wants. And I'm not sure I've ever had that.

DELILAH
(*not unkindly*)
That sounds insane. Like something an insane person would say.

JENNIFER
Insane things can be true.

DELILAH
How do you know my *dad* isn't taking advantage of you?

JENNIFER
It's true. Maybe he's marrying me for my pots of money. Or for constant access to my ancient cats. Or my tiny bedsit in Brighton.

DELILAH
You've got an apartment in Brighton?

JENNIFER
Who's taking advantage of you, Delilah?

DELILAH
No one.

JENNIFER
. . .
All right. Well. If no one was taking advantage of me I think I'd stop to ask myself what precisely no one wants. And if no one wanted something I didn't feel comfortable providing, I'd find a polite way to say—to no one—that I'm grateful for everything but we'll have to proceed in a way that doesn't involve my feeling compromised, even if no one believes no one's in the wrong at all.

(**Delilah** *stares at her.*)

Just flatter them. And you can get away with anything.

DELILAH
It sounds like you *have* been taken advantage of.

JENNIFER
I've just been in the world for a long time. With my eyes open. That's all.

DELILAH
(*to the audience*)
So that night I wrote Greenhill an email thanking him for all of his help
and mentioning that my boyfriend who happens to be an Olympic boxing hopeful
is also a fan and last weekend we bought a copy of Greenhill's book
Bodies of Work and Bodies in Space and spent
Saturday night reading passages from it out loud to each other.
. . . And it actually worked.

JENNIFER
(*to the audience*)

When we left the toilet, John asked what happened to
my dress—
was I quite all right? And I said I was fine; I was great, actually.
Not admitting that for the first time I felt a bit, I don't
know . . . parental?
Doling out advice without letting on that's what I was doing.

DELILAH
I see Jennifer a week or two later when I go over to do my
laundry.

JENNIFER
Oh, let me take my things out of the machine so you can—

DELILAH
Thank you.

JENNIFER
It's no problem.

DELILAH
No. I actually meant ... for before.

JENNIFER
For before?

DELILAH
Like for helping me.

JENNIFER
How did I help you before?

DELILAH
With that situation I was in ...

(**Jennifer** *is blank*)

DELILAH
That situation with no one.

JENNIFER
Oh! ...Well ...That was no problem either.
If anything is improved in your life then I'm very happy
and also certain I had nothing to do with it.

DELILAH
And I leave their house with this sort of warm feeling,
which is strange because it's cold out, colder than London
ever gets, and by the time I get home, well to Tracy's place,
I can't feel my fingers
and am therefore not too enthused when Tracy
wants to go up on the roof after hearing what we assume
are fireworks.
But once we're up there it's clear we're too late
and I start to pull her back into the house, into the warm house,
when I hear someone call my name
but I turn around and Tracy's like: wazzup bitch
and blows vape smoke in my face.
So yeah she hadn't heard it.
And she goes downstairs.
And I'm alone up there and the whole city seems just *silent*
like everyone and everything's been put on pause
but not everyone it turns out because nonchalantly,
out from behind the chimney thing, walks, you know . . . my mother.

(*Beat*)

We looked at each other.
She looked the same. The way she did when she . . .

JENNIFER
All right, I'll tell the truth.
I knew about Delilah's troubles with her tutor.
I have a problem—I've had it since I was a girl—
a problem that might generously be termed "snooping"
but has perhaps more to do with curiosity

and, I fear, a touch of madness
and the almost always borne-out assumption
that others who aren't me lead more interesting lives.
And the morning of the wedding, Delilah left her phone
on the sideboard beside the continental breakfast
so of course I took a quick peek. It wasn't even locked.
Immediately I was outraged.
What was this "Professor Greenhill" thinking?
He ought to be ashamed of himself, a grown man;
to myself I made the joke that he should go and find
a green hill, climb up it and never come down.

DELILAH
She was in the dress of hers that was
my favorite, this long dark dress that she'd wear
with these platform boots that I loved
and this, among other things, made me think:
don't be an idiot, Delilah—
what you're seeing is unquestionably in your head.
Which is when she said: *"I'm not in your head,*
sweetie. Not a small square of London night
whipped into some kind of blue illusion.
No, I'm your mother's spirit, visiting because I missed you.
Because I've been watching and this seemed
like the right time to say hello."
(**Delilah** *is open-mouthed and in shock*)

JENNIFER
I don't know if she knows I snooped
but the next time I see her
Delilah is angry with me again.
And because she seems angry I get a bit rattled
and on impulse offer her a lovely
but useless silver platter we'd been gifted for the wedding
that I'd been
thinking of returning.
(*to* **Delilah**)

Why don't you exchange it at the shop and get something
nice for yourself! I think they sell jewelry. You could get a
necklace or some earrings.

DELILAH
Earrings.

JENNIFER
(to the audience)
I want to say: perhaps some smaller ones
that look less like they're engaged in a boxing match
with her face.

DELILAH
I don't understand—you want me to do what exactly?

JENNIFER
(to the audience)
As though I'd asked her to dispose
of a few dead bodies that just so happened to be decaying in
the garden.

DELILAH
You're asking me to return this for you?

JENNIFER
No, no, no. To return it and get something for yourself. Get
yourself a present.

DELILAH
This is instead of you putting in some time and thought and
actually getting me a present.

JENNIFER
Oh—is it your birthday soon?

DELILAH
No.

JENNIFER
Then why would I get you a present?

DELILAH
I don't know! You just said I should get myself a present!

JENNIFER
Would you like me to get you a present, Delilah?

DELILAH
Nah I'm good. Thanks.

JENNIFER
(*to the audience*)
I mean really.

DELILAH
(*to the audience*)
You can't *ask* someone if they want a present! Who does that?

JENNIFER
(*to the audience*)
And so I exchanged the platter for a slightly more useful, if less beautiful, bowl and every time I saw it, filled with bananas or what have you, I'd think to myself "this should be a necklace, but somehow it's a bowl."

DELILAH
(*defending herself*)
I was distracted! To be fair, I was being a dick to *everyone* around me.

JENNIFER
I try again—because it seems important to John.
It makes me wonder if maybe *this* is what
he sees in me—what he needs from me.
If maybe it's less about "love" than finding
someone who will at least *try* to help

with some of the more intractable issues,
(*not really convinced*)
and maybe that's okay.

DELILAH
I couldn't tell anyone
in part because she said: *"Delilah you can't tell anyone.
If you tell anyone, I won't be able to come back."*
Like I'm starting to learn the rules of this game
and it turns out there's not much wiggle room.
Also there's the not insignificant
question of whether I'm going insane.
I mean, this is what an insane person does, right?
Goes up to the roof every night, talks to a ghost
for a few hours, gets very little sleep
and does it all over again the next night.

JENNIFER
I ask Delilah if she might be willing
to meet me for a tea and at first
she doesn't respond
and then when I follow up
she does respond, but it's quite terse,
as in all she writes is "no."
So that sends something of a message, doesn't it?

DELILAH
But I can't bail on my mom, and I don't want to;
it always might be the last time, just the way that
was true when she was alive, only I didn't know it,
and she's talking to me like I'm an adult, which we never
got to do when she was . . . I mean, she wants to know
my opinion about capitalism and art and dad's new beard
(*she gives it a thumbs down*)
and *Dancing with the Stars*, which I tell her is called
Strictly Come Dancing over here, which seems to upset her?
But really she's unimpressed by most things except . . . me;

it's crazy: she still looks at me like she used to, when I was
little and she'd watch me act out the plays my older cousin
Tanya made up, where Tanya always cast herself as the lead
and me as the dog
or the mute sister, but still my mom would just gaze at me,
like she couldn't believe I was hers.

JENNIFER
In the meantime there is something brewing.
Talk of a virus that's starting to snake its way out into the
world. China and now cruise ships where people are being
kept in their little rooms like the mice we all truly know
ourselves to be.

DELILAH
And she's telling me these stories I never knew like *"your
dad's brother owes him four hundred and fifty pounds which, with
interest, is more than a thousand at this point,
and that's what your dad will say if you ask him."*
So the next time I see him I'm like
how's uncle Frank? And dad says: fine, same
as always. And then I ask if he owes him
any money and dad's eyes get wide
and he says "that bastard has owed
me four hundred and fifty pounds for
twenty-five years now, which means with interest it'd be more
than a thousand."
And then he's like "when did I tell you about that?"
and I shrug.

JENNIFER
My mother would have said "people are just working
themselves
into a lather, Jennifer"—I can almost hear her.
(She enjoyed suggesting that most human responses were
hopelessly extreme,

this from a person who would lose her head
if I put the wrong pan in the dishwasher.)

DELILAH
And she's wearing this crazy hat that's
not something she would've worn in a million
years.
I ask her about it and she's just like,
"you don't like it?" and I didn't know
you could hurt a ghost's feelings
but I also didn't know there *were* ghosts
til just recently so I guess you could say I'm on a steep
learning curve.

JENNIFER
But I do wish we'd been able to go away together. Me and John.
And he says we will, we just need to wait now for all of this virus "stuff"
to pass. It's not safe to travel, he says. And I think to myself, even to Brighton, crumbling old Brighton, for a weekend by the sea?

DELILAH
One day, *out of nowhere,* she's like *"Okay so this is gonna sound…*
but do you remember your 2nd grade teacher, Mrs. Mathis? She was saccharine sweet—
she had that little sing-songy voice so that even when she was telling me
you might need to be <u>left back</u> if you had one more pee accident –
you really couldn't stop peeing that year –
it sounded like she was saying something nice and for a second I could forget
that I wanted to slap the shit out of her. And Delilah, I just have this feeling
there's something Mrs. Mathis-y about Jennifer."

"She doesn't have a sing-songy voice," I say. And my
mother's like
*"no, but she's kind. On the surface at least. And that can reel
you in when you're not looking."* "Jennifer's just weird,"
I say,
"she talks to her cats." But then my mother gives me
this look
that's like deeply forlorn and I'm like, "I won't get reeled in,
I promise."

JENNIFER
But it's February and who wants to go to the foggy seaside
anyway, so I let it go.
And I start to see him less and less.

DELILAH
At this point I haven't been to class in weeks,
and I get this email from the registrar asking
if I want to make up the exams I've missed
but my mother says *"don't worry so much
about school;
aren't we having fun?"* and I say of course
but also start to wonder if maybe
this isn't *exactly* my mother, and it's somehow even more
disconcerting than discovering the ghost of my mother
to discover that that ghost isn't wholly her
because in life she was very focused on my doing well in school;
she wouldn't let me stay home sick, not even if I had the
kind of fever
when you're really supposed to stay home sick.
And all of a sudden I want my dad, like desperately.
The next time I see him I almost tell him everything
but he's so harried that it doesn't seem like the right moment,
which annoys me; apparently there's some like lethal
virus that's gonna kill everyone, and all the doctors are
freaking out
and I can't help it—I blame Jennifer.
So yeah, when she "asks me to tea" I decline, okay?

And when she asks me a third time, I go—
but only to make things worse.

JENNIFER
Well hello Delilah—it's certainly been a while.

DELILAH
Hello Jennifer it has indeed been a while.

(*Silence*)

JENNIFER
And how've you been?

DELILAH
I've been just fine.

JENNIFER
Well that's wonderful.

DELILAH
It really is.

JENNIFER
Yes.

DELILAH
And you?

JENNIFER
Oh gosh. Me?

DELILAH
That bad?

JENNIFER
No, not at all. I don't know why I said it that way. Things are fine with me.

DELILAH
Yeah? My dad's not too busy these days?

JENNIFER
Well everyone in the whole NHS is busy these days.

DELILAH
Even you.

JENNIFER
I daresay I have more work now than I've ever had.

DELILAH
A lot of paperwork?

JENNIFER
It is. Richard—that's my boss—says we are preparing for the storm, like the crew of a ship that doesn't know where it's headed, so must ready ourselves for anything.

DELILAH
(*saluting*)
Thank you for your service to our country. Or should I say your country.

JENNIFER
It's your country too.

DELILAH
In what sense?

JENNIFER
Well, you're a citizen, aren't you?

DELILAH
Actually, I think my British passport is about to expire.

JENNIFER
Oh, you should renew it. Right away.

You don't want to be caught out anywhere right now.
I think people are starting to feel quite vulnerable.
(*an admission*)
I think *I'm* starting to feel quite . . . vulnerable.

DELILAH
Because you're old.

JENNIFER
Thank you, Delilah. Yes.

DELILAH
And with my dad so busy it's like you're alone all over again.
Does any part of you wonder if my dad's absence has more
to do with you than with his work? Like maybe there's a
reason you were alone for so long.

(**Jennifer** *looks at* **Delilah,** *then decides she can't carry on; she stands to go.*)

DELILAH
What are you doing?

JENNIFER
Precisely what you'd like me to, I think.

(**Jennifer** *puts a twenty-pound note on the table.*)

This should cover our coffees.

(*She starts to leave and then stops.*)

Aren't you going to ask me not to go?

DELILAH
No.

JENNIFER
(*to the audience*)
I mean, we all have our limits.
I tell John I won't see her anymore
and he says he understands but clearly he's devastated,
which is almost worse than if he'd yelled or begged me to reconsider.
And evidently he tells Delilah to make amends
because she starts calling the house but you know,
I'm no doormat.

DELILAH
Hi Jennifer, do you have a minute?

JENNIFER
Is this Delilah?

DELILAH
You know it's Delilah.

JENNIFER
Oh well, I don't have a minute, I'm sorry.

DELILAH
And she, like, hangs up.

JENNIFER
Which didn't feel terrible, I must admit.

DELILAH
I couldn't believe Jennifer was acting so childish.
She, like, wouldn't talk to me.

JENNIFER
Also everything at the time was so…topsy turvy.
The whole world seemed in the process of shutting down,
like the world was a concert and suddenly the musicians
were needed elsewhere.

DELILAH
And my mother's like, *"come on, it's probably for the best"*
and out of genuine curiosity, I'm like "why?
When this person had seemed to be more or less on
my side
and does boast the minor benefit of being, well...alive . . . "
Which is when she laughs like I haven't heard
her laugh in years: *"Is looking at your email
the behavior of someone on your side?"*
and I say: Jennifer doesn't look at my email
and my mother says *"you wanna bet?"*
and then I get kind of furious, like aren't
there more important things to discuss
than Jennifer? Aren't there people dying
of mysterious diseases and fighting for justice
and to, like, save the planet
and also if we're focused on my personal life
isn't the matter of why *you're* here
more pressing than anything to do with
Jennifer, like if you had the *choice* to come back
why didn't you come sooner?
Didn't you miss me?
At which point she *disappears*.

JENNIFER
And then . . . Delilah *moved into* my house.

DELILAH
Not immediately. I mean, I waited three months
for my mom to come back. And she didn't.
She didn't. Like, I couldn't even...
And Tracy was being low-key toxic
and plucking her eyebrows really aggressively
so eventually I was just like "I'm out"
and Tracy left to go stay with
her parents in Durham
and my dad was like . . . okay, yeah, sure,
that'll be really nice, come stay with us,

but I guess he didn't run it by
Jennifer?

JENNIFER
Well this is certainly a surprise.

DELILAH
A good one or a bad one?

JENNIFER
Just a surprise. But it's fine. I'll get the guest bedroom
ready for you.

DELILAH
The ghost bedroom?

JENNIFER
What?

DELILAH
Sorry, what?

JENNIFER
Not that you're a guest here.

DELILAH
Not that you're a ghost.

JENNIFER
I'm saying you're not a guest.
This is your home too, of course.

DELILAH
You say all the right things, Jennifer.

JENNIFER
Isn't it funny, I have no idea what day it is.
Or even the time of day.

DELILAH
It's 5 o'clock. And it's Thursday.

JENNIFER
Isn't it always just.

DELILAH
I'm gonna unpack.

JENNIFER
And seeing as it's 5 o'clock I'll start thinking about something for dinner.

DELILAH
I start thinking about dinner right after I eat lunch. Sometimes even before lunch.
Also I was shitting you. It's 3 o'clock. But it might as well be 5.

JENNIFER
You were "shitting me."

DELILAH
That's what I just said.

JENNIFER
And that means . . . lying?

DELILAH
Yeah basically. Or, like, teasing.

JENNIFER
I never went in for teasing.

DELILAH
No, the person being teased usually doesn't.

JENNIFER
No.

(**Delilah** *turns to leave*)

JENNIFER
(*abruptly, to keep* **Delilah** *in the room, and also to get back at her*)
Hey . . . how's uni?

DELILAH
What?

JENNIFER
I wondered how you've been finding it. At uni. These days.

DELILAH
Why do you ask it like that?

JENNIFER
Like what?

DELILAH
Like something's wrong.

JENNIFER
I didn't.

(**Delilah** *stares at her*)

JENNIFER
(*to the audience*)
I'd had another little peek at her email
and saw that the registrar had written about making up her exams.
I'm not proud of it, of course. You have to believe
that I'm not proud of it. And to look at me, you wouldn't think:
computer whiz. Expert hacker. But I do have a touch of genius
when it comes to these things.
I really can get into almost anything—

DELILAH
(*cutting her off*)
Okay so I'm gonna unpack.
(*She turns and then turns back.*)
Oh, and I assume you don't mind if I play music and listen to true crime podcasts and keep bizarre hours, making an unfortunate amount of noise when I come in and out in the middle of the night, right? It got to be a little too much for Trevor—he was my roommate—but I figured it would be fine to do at home. (*Goading her.*) With my *family*.

JENNIFER
(*deciding whether or not to engage*)
. . . It sounds like fun.

DELILAH
What does?

JENNIFER
Your life.

DELILAH
Oh—no. No one should have FOMO for my life.

JENNIFER
(*to the audience*)
I had no good answer to that
because I didn't have any clue what "FOMO" meant
so when Delilah went to her room
I sat at the computer
and typed it out, first spelling
it in all the wrong ways before
finally landing on its meaning
and feeling immediately
a shock of recognition, as though
hearing my name called in a room
I'd thought was empty.

For instance, for years I'd hear about people's
weekend trips and skiing holidays, nights out dancing
until two in the morning—and wonder, despite myself, whether
I shouldn't be doing those same sorts of things.
(*happily amazed*)
And it turns out—that's FOMO!

DELILAH
In the afternoons, Jennifer goes to Tescos,
which is when I head to the kitchen
and grab bags of crisps and make my sandwich
and take a whole cut cantaloupe if there is one because why not, right?
And one day, for reasons I don't really understand,
I grab Jennifer's honey pot
but I have so much in my arms that on the way
upstairs I drop everything
and some of the honey spills on the carpet
and my sandwich is full of fuzz now
and by the time I get to my room I feel like I've
really been through something
and basically need to rest for the entire afternoon.

JENNIFER
But when you really think about FOMO,
and I have been,
you start to wonder if it derives from some
prehistoric instinct, the impulse
that perhaps you should be somewhere else
or with other people in order to survive.
Which means that now, it's essentially defunct
like . . . the little toe of emotional responses,
which would in turn explain why I actually
have no interest in doing the things that I give
myself a hard time for missing out on—
why, when it comes down to it,
I'd much prefer to stay in, always.

With a book and my cup of tea with honey,
which strangely has gone missing of late.

(**Jennifer** *goes into* **Delilah's** *room.*)

JENNIFER
Hi Delilah—

DELILAH
You could knock.

JENNIFER
I just wondered if you'd possibly seen my little honey pot.
It's in the shape of a bear. It was my mother's.

DELILAH
Nope, sorry.

JENNIFER
Okay.
(*turning, then turning back*)
It's just I could've sworn there was a little honey on the stairs;
I leaned down and put my nose to the carpet . . . and I smelled something; I'm sure I did.

DELILAH
Sniffing carpets is weird. Maybe don't do that, or don't tell people you've done it.

JENNIFER
So you have no idea.

DELILAH
None.
Just as I assume you have no idea how to get into my email.

JENNIFER
What are you talking about??

DELILAH
(*to the audience*)
For a while after that I didn't want to leave my room. Not even to get food
because it might mean running into Jennifer in the kitchen and having to, like, chat.
Also: I didn't want to leave any of my devices unattended.

JENNIFER
(*to the audience*)
Is it possible that I myself moved the honey pot?
 . . . No, I don't think so, and John doesn't drink tea
and is also never here (sometimes I wonder,
did I marry a ghost? After all so many are ghosts these
days, London itself a ghost town, Tottenham Court
Road as quiet as a country lane). In fact, I realized
(with some dismay) that my discovery of FOMO was already outdated—
it too a ghost from another time when people went out and did things.

DELILAH
The next Wednesday or maybe it was Thursday,
I was about to go to sleep for the night, even though it was only
4 pm because why not; I mean, my ghost mother
had pretty definitively ghosted me—and I'd already
watched *Love Island* and every episode of *The Wire*— twice—
if I'm honest I was feeling nostalgic for Baltimore where
I'd done this honors program for eighth graders. It was the summer
before my mother died. On the way home she took me
to the Baltimore Museum of Art and showed me these carvings
that illustrated regular people doing quietly heroic things,
which was, she felt, one of the best things a piece of art can do.

JENNIFER
(*to the audience*)
I have never claimed to be the most perceptive person in
the world but I *can* tell

when someone needs their space. Also I wasn't positive
Delilah was eating anything?
Which meant that against every instinct drilled into me by
my mother
having to do with food and where in a house it ought to be
eaten
I brought all of Delilah's snacks up to the landing outside
her room so she wouldn't
have to go far to get to them. I made a little shelf
for her crisps and cheesy Wotsits and those sour peach
sweeties
that make my lips feel strange.

DELILAH
I smelled them immediately. Those Wotsits.
For a minute I thought it was my mom—back again—but
then something told me, no;
this was Jennifer. It was the way she'd stacked the books on
the shelf to make
room for the crisps. She'd made this kind of anally neat
pyramid with them.
And I had to go back into my room because I thought I
might cry.
Instead I ate a bag of salt and vinegar crisps and started to
turn on the TV—
but then I changed my mind.

(*to* **Jennifer**)

So do you want to watch something?

JENNIFER
What?

DELILAH
I was just wondering if you wanted to watch something.
With me.

JENNIFER
You mean a show on the telly?

DELILAH
Yeah. Or a movie.

JENNIFER
A movie. Gracious.

DELILAH
Why, do you have something better to do? You look like you're just sitting there.

JENNIFER
I was thinking.

DELILAH
Well by all means, carry on.

JENNIFER
No—I do want to watch something.

DELILAH
(*to the audience*)
And then it took us about an hour to choose what turned out to be a twenty-seven-minute documentary.

JENNIFER
(*to the audience*)
Delilah vetoed *everything*. Everything was either boring, or "sus" or she'd seen it already or she wasn't interested. I couldn't even get her to watch Miss Marple!

DELILAH
(*to the audience*)
She wanted me to watch something called Miss Marple. How sus is that.

JENNIFER
(*to the audience*)
But then we settled in. Just two women on a sofa with nowhere to go.

DELILAH
(*to the audience*)
The documentary we watched was about rhinos.
Like it turns out there are only two Northern White rhinoceroses
left in the entire world. *Functionally Extinct* was the name of the movie,
which refers to the fact that the two remaining rhinos are female
so there's no way they can reproduce.

JENNIFER
Well, that was really something. I didn't know anything about rhinos, did you?

DELILAH
(*to the audience*)
The even sadder thing is that they're actually a mother and daughter. Those last two rhinos.

JENNIFER
I found it quite moving too.

DELILAH
(*she is, a little*)
I'm not crying or anything.

JENNIFER
No, of course not.

DELILAH
But yeah . . . it was sad. How it's just the end of the line for them.

JENNIFER
Hey, it happens to the best of us. We all come eventually to the end of the line.

DELILAH
Well, this is really cheering me up. Thanks.

JENNIFER
I'm sorry. My father used to say "que sera sera" whenever I asked him a serious question. It always got on my nerves. I wanted him to have a better answer. Or to know more.

DELILAH
What did you ask him?

JENNIFER
Oh I don't know. Maybe it was like the song. Will I be pretty. Will I be rich.

DELILAH
Will I store medical records.

JENNIFER
I don't think I asked him that.

DELILAH
What was he like?

JENNIFER
Oh . . . he was quiet. You really had to prod him to get him talking. Sometimes you could forget he was in the room. Not like my mother, who took up a fair bit of space.

DELILAH
(*bold and vulnerable at once*)
Are there things you wish you'd done with your life, that you didn't do?

(**Jennifer** *looks at her, doesn't say anything*)

DELILAH
Sorry.

JENNIFER
No, it's fine.

DELILAH
So do you ever see them? Your parents?

JENNIFER
What was that?

DELILAH
Do they visit you?

JENNIFER
Um, no. I mean, not with any regularity.

DELILAH
Oh. Well that's okay. Sometimes it's more trouble than it's worth.
For one thing, when they stop coming it can be very hurtful.
Anyway, thanks for the movie.
And the crisps.

JENNIFER
(*to the audience*)
I must say: I wonder about the vast gulf that is all I don't know about Delilah.
. . . And then whether I'm even allowed to wonder about it.

DELILAH
(*to the audience*)
And then—*she comes back.*
I'm up on Jennifer's roof and she just appears,
wearing a Covid mask, one of those beautiful cloth ones that look ripped
from, like, upholstery at Versailles and probably cost
more than anything I own. "Why are you wearing that?" I ask
and she's like "how was movie night?"

JENNIFER
I mean, maybe she writes poetry. Or dreams in rhyme.
Maybe she's one of those people for whom sounds make colors
or colors make sounds. I don't know.

DELILAH
And I want to be mad at her for disappearing like that
but instead, pathetically, I'm just like "where were you?"
and she says, *"you know I can't tell you that,"*
which I didn't know (how would I know ghost rules
she hasn't shared yet) and even more pathetically I say
"that's fine; I'm just happy to see you again" because I am;
and I can tell she wants to touch me but that's not
something we can do; all of a sudden she says she loved me
before I was born and she will love me into eternity
and she's sorry she died; she didn't want to. And I say
I know that.
And any anger I might've been harboring is like a
boat put out to sea.
But then she changes the subject.
"So what were you thinking, moving in here?"
and I worry she's upset with me, but she says:
*"no, it's brilliant. I don't know why I didn't think of it myself.
Also you should get a gun."*

JENNIFER
And the not knowing
makes me feel so . . . helpless
which is my least favorite feeling, really,
like when my mother died—and I just sat there,
dumbly, beside her bed holding her hand;
I couldn't save her.

DELILAH
And I am . . . I mean, I am *gob-smacked* . . .
My mother never believed in *guns*; we marched
against guns, against war, against you name it . . .
But she says there's just something about Jennifer.
And I say: that her shampoo smells like eggs?
She says Jennifer knows what she's trying to do.
What is she trying to do? Steal my Netflix password so she can watch
more old lady mysteries set in foggy seaside towns?
"No, Delilah, she's dangerous. You need to take this seriously.
If you value continuing to have me on your roof
and in your heart, that is."

JENNIFER
How ashamed I was—and still am. And here it is,
happening again, because at night
Delilah has started screaming in her sleep and

JENNIFER AND DELILAH
I lie in bed

JENNIFER
Eyes open, entirely incapable of—

DELILAH
And all I can see behind my eyes every night
are those two lady rhinos
like, stomping along, shaking the earth—
this place that has been their home

since eternity, only now it feels like it's closing in
on them.
And the daughter rhino ponders this,
not realizing she's slowed down (it turns
out rhinos can't really think and run at the same time)
and when she comes to, the mother rhino is way ahead;
she can't catch up; she tries but the harder she runs
the farther apart they get. And the day is ending.
That part of the day when you can't really tell if it's day
or night,
and then shots ring out in the blue air;
the daughter watches as the mother goes down,
and the earth vibrates as she falls; it shudders
with the sadness of the mountains and the deserts.
The daughter wants desperately to be there, to lick
her mother's salty cheek, or make the boisterous noise
she knows would summon their ancestors to carry
her mother's soul away on the wind.
But then—
she's hit too—she's hit, she's hit—it's over.
(**Delilah** *is speechless for a moment, bereft*)
And before long—running into focus, as though to claim
what's rightfully his,
is this grinning man with a gun; only it isn't a man—
it's me.

JENNIFER
And John is never home;
he's doing all-night shifts now,
which terrifies me because the air is full of demons
shooting their arrows indiscriminately;
and Delilah is screaming
and I'm not her mother or even a person
she likes
but I am here
so finally one night I open her door—

(**Delilah** *screams*)

JENNIFER
It's only me—it's me. I heard you yell, and—

DELILAH
There was a man, did you see him?

JENNIFER
What man?

DELILAH
Use your eyes! Are you blind? Did you see him or not?

JENNIFER
See who?

DELILAH
Or do you think it was me? The man??

JENNIFER
You're sleeping. You were screaming and it woke me up.

DELILAH
(*a sudden realization*)
Or maybe it was . . . you.

JENNIFER
Sorry?

DELILAH
(*putting things together*)
She says you're dangerous.

JENNIFER
Who says that.

DELILAH
Who do you think??

JENNIFER
I wouldn't like to guess.

DELILAH
If I had to, I'd guess *you* killed the rhinos.

JENNIFER
From the documentary??

DELILAH
And they were the last ones.

JENNIFER
Delilah, you're asleep right now. You're dreaming.
For one thing you're not a man and I'm not a—

(**Jennifer** *touches her arm lightly;* **Delilah**'s *dream—or whatever it was—breaks. She staggers backwards)*

DELILAH
(*confused, upset*)
Why are you, like . . . touching me? It's weird.

JENNIFER
I'm sorry—I barely touched you. I just . . . you seemed to need waking and . . .

DELILAH
I can decide what I need, okay?

(*Beat*)

JENNIFER
(*to the audience*)
I just . . . I didn't know what to do.
I thought . . . well I don't know what I thought.
After all, one day I'd spy my mother's
slim jade vase, the one she used to put a
single stalk in at the start of spring,
and then it'd be gone, and I'd wonder

if maybe the vase never existed at all. Or if it
just went the way of the honey pot
and the reading glasses and the necklace stand
and the bookend in the shape of
an elephant's tusk that my mother would
joke was real; she'd say it was the most
memorable part of the safari, when she
coaxed the elephant into giving up its tusk,
but of course she'd never been on safari;
this was just the kind of thing that amused
her: coming up with little stories,
lives we might have led
in some other, more forgiving, or more
thrilling, universe.

DELILAH
(*to the audience*)
You could almost *hear* life passing.
It made a little song.
My room. The hallway. The roof. The kitchen.
That was the rhythm I got stuck in
sometime in October

JENNIFER
. . . or maybe it was November. It was always difficult to say.
At some point the country "locks down" again
and so again I stop swimming my laps at the aquatic centre
and again do all my work from home,
our homes that become stifling once more
and seem to exist to hold us back as opposed to holding
us close at the end of a long day, as they used to.

DELILAH
I said I don't want to talk about that.

JENNIFER
It's just that you don't seem to be doing much in the way of
your studies.

DELILAH
How would you know?

JENNIFER
Delilah . . . did you . . . did you maybe—drop out?

DELILAH
I said I don't want to talk about it, okay!?

JENNIFER
(*to the audience*)
For reasons you can surmise, I knew for a fact that she'd dropped out. Or taken a leave or whatever it was called.

DELILAH
You shouldn't even be in my room.

JENNIFER
Well, I was looking for some of my things.
Some of my mother's things, to be precise.
Not knowing where they are I feel a bit . . . unsettled, you see.
Or *more* than a bit unsettled if I'm being honest.

DELILAH
This is *my* room.

JENNIFER
Well, it's *my* house.

DELILAH
Oh is that how you want to play it?

JENNIFER
Um. No.
I don't know.
How *should* I play it?
I'm just trying to be nice.

DELILAH
News flash: it's not working.

JENNIFER
(*to the audience*)
I don't know.
I don't know.
I didn't know what to do.
My friend Sarah said give her time, so . . .

DELILAH
And my mother won't stop going on about how Jennifer is overplaying
her hand, asking me about uni and all that; "it's not her place," she keeps saying.

JENNIFER
. . . and then it was Christmas time.

DELILAH
For days, she won't let me sleep, and finally I'm so tired I'm just like:
okay, yes, it wasn't her place—

JENNIFER
Or the time when, in a normal year, Christmas would occur.

DELILAH
Okay—it wasn't her place.
It wasn't her place . . .

JENNIFER
John is home, *finally*—
and I put up decorations which I'd never done before
but it felt like everyone needed a little cheering up, didn't it.

DELILAH
She says she's gonna get me a Christmas present,
one that'll "help me" with Jennifer.

JENNIFER
I bought a little plastic tree that somehow still smells like pine
and was of two minds about a tiny Santa figurine
but then got it because if not now when, right?

DELILAH
I ask how it'll help and she says it wouldn't be fair to tell me
because a really good present has to be a surprise.

JENNIFER
And we make mulled wine and wear our slippers
and try to play our parts but John can't hide how sad he is
that Delilah doesn't come to dinner and I feel somehow sure
the house has stolen my mother's things, slipped them
into a pocket because I didn't deserve them anymore,
having proven myself
perhaps *uniquely* dreadful at, well, being a daughter, and a wife, and now
almost-mother to someone who clearly needed one.

DELILAH
But it wasn't a surprise for long. There's a box
under the tree the night before Christmas eve;
it's wrapped really neatly
and I take it to my room and tear it open;
at first I don't see anything and I think:
maybe that's the best a ghost can do: an empty box;
but then, there it is, and gingerly,
like really gingerly, I take it out
and . . . it's a gun.

JENNIFER
Eventually John says the wine has gone to his head
and he's going to go to sleep. He's been feeling
a bit peaky lately; he really should rest.
But before he starts upstairs he stands on the bottom step

and says: "I know you want an explanation,
but I honestly don't think it matters why, Jennifer;
I just love you; I love everything about you, truly,
and maybe that can be enough?"
I want to cry he's so earnest. And it is, in fact,
a moment I never forget. Because . . . shortly thereafter:

DELILAH
It feels completely unfair.

JENNIFER
Did you hear me, Delilah? Your dad's gone to hospital.

DELILAH
(*to the audience*)
It feels completely unfair
that in all likelihood one of those rhinos will die before the other
and then there will be a loneliness like none that's
ever existed before.

JENNIFER
He went in early this morning. He has a . . . blood disorder.
It's serious, I'm afraid. He said it's like his own body is
attacking itself.

DELILAH
Like being brutally attacked from the inside.

JENNIFER
Did you hear me?

DELILAH
I hear you. My father is sick.

JENNIFER
(*about her plastic bag*)
And what's that you have there?

DELILAH
What, my bag?

JENNIFER
(*to the audience*)
And because of the moment in which
we find ourselves
I can't visit and Delilah can't visit;
so instead we end up on Christmas Eve in this strange vigil
next to that stupid plastic tree
and that stupid figurine Santa
and oh how I wish I'd never bought any of it.

DELILAH
It's just a bag.

JENNIFER
Well, do you want to put it down?

DELILAH
No.

JENNIFER
What's in it exactly?

DELILAH
A gun.

JENNIFER
A gun?

DELILAH
That's what I said.

JENNIFER
Like a real . . .

DELILAH
Why wouldn't it be real?

JENNIFER
And um . . . should I ask, like . . . why it is that you have a . . .

DELILAH
Probably not.

JENNIFER
All right. And are you planning for it to come *out of* the bag at any point?

DELILAH
Not planning on it, no.

JENNIFER
Is there a particular reason why you have it?

DELILAH
I'm pretty sure it's because my mother doesn't like you.

JENNIFER
Oh, *she* got you the gun?

DELILAH
For Christmas.

JENNIFER
For Christmas. She got you this gun for Christmas.

DELILAH
Is there an echo in here, or . . .

JENNIFER
I'm just trying to understand.

DELILAH
Well maybe you should do less trying and more understanding.

JENNIFER
. . . Delilah, your father is very sick.

DELILAH
I'm aware.

JENNIFER
We should get the results of the biopsy tonight. Any minute now, really. So . . . we have to be thinking of him. Praying.

DELILAH
Why, do you actually believe in God?

JENNIFER
Do you?

DELILAH
I asked first.

JENNIFER
I believe in prayer.

DELILAH
When my mother began to visit me I started to feel more sure of the existence of God. Or something like God.

(*Beat.* **Jennifer** *tries to decide how to respond.*)

JENNIFER
Can you say more about . . . her visits.

DELILAH
Well, at first she was a pretty placid ghost. But lately she's gotten a little more . . . I don't know . . . insistent.

JENNIFER
Insistent about what?

DELILAH
You, mostly.

JENNIFER
Me.

DELILAH
Really it would just be better if you left me and my dad alone.

JENNIFER
Delilah, you know I can't do that.

DELILAH
Actually you can.

JENNIFER
Your father is my husband.

DELILAH
Which makes zero sense.

JENNIFER
And why's that?

DELILAH
Just like, looking at you compared to my mom.

JENNIFER
Well in that particular comparison only one of us is alive, so.

JENNIFER
Can we please just have a reasonable conversa—

DELILAH
You can't have an actual conversation. You can't even say what you really want for dinner.

JENNIFER
What are you talking about??

DELILAH
Do you think my dad is gonna die??

JENNIFER
What? No. I mean, no. We're praying so he won't.

DELILAH
I'm asking a simple question. Do you think he will or don't you?

JENNIFER
No. I don't.

DELILAH
You wouldn't be okay if he died—he's literally all you have.

JENNIFER
He's not going to die.

DELILAH
But you don't know that! It happens! People die. All the time.

JENNIFER
You're right—you're right. And, um . . . how do you . . . feel about that?

DELILAH
(*trying to hold back tears, failing*)
How do I *feel*?

JENNIFER
Can you tell me? Not because I think I can help you.
Necessarily.
Just because . . . it might be good to get it off your chest.
And because . . . I want to know.
Because I . . . want to know you.

DELILAH
. . . Oh. *This* is what she . . . Shit. I'm such a . . .
(*She realizes she no longer has the bag*)

JENNIFER
Delilah, I'm not trying to be your . . . How would I even know how to do that??

DELILAH
(*tumbling out, in a rant*)
I don't know I don't know—

JENNIFER
Will you please just sit down—

DELILAH
Sit down? How could I . . . ? (*starting to speak, almost to herself*)
She was *alive*. My mother. She was—everything. And then she was just – gone. Only it wasn't possible she was gone because she was enormous.

(*voice cracking*)

But you. You have cats. You talk to them. And you're old. When I'm with you I have to think about being old. I mean, what is your life? You never laugh. You look at me like I'm from—like I'm—I just, I don't understand how he could have married you. You're an island. You're nobody—

(**Jennifer** *abruptly envelops her in a hug. Eventually* **Delilah** *hugs her back. Soon they sink to the floor.* **Delilah** *holds the bag open, upside down. It's empty.*)

DELILAH
No.
No no no that's not . . .

JENNIFER
Delilah.

DELILAH
It was there.

JENNIFER
I believe you.

DELILAH
No you don't.

JENNIFER
I do, actually.

DELILAH
But that's not possible.

(**Delilah**'s *eyes fill with tears*)

That's not possible.

JENNIFER
Do you remember how I told you I used to take those step classes?

(She nods)

Well, do you want to know why I stopped?

DELILAH
Not really.

JENNIFER
It was because I went into hospital.

DELILAH
Why.

JENNIFER
My only friend, Sarah, got pregnant.
I was thirty-eight. And I think I felt like I was gonna be . . .

DELILAH
What?

JENNIFER
I don't know.

(quietly)

Alone forever?
So I just . . . stopped sleeping.
I mean, days were nights and nights were days. It was
evening all afternoon, which is a line from a poem I've
otherwise forgotten. There was music playing and I couldn't
work out where it was coming from. Always the same
song – that one by the Monkees—you know, um:
Cheer up, sleepy Jean . . .

DELILAH
No.

JENNIFER
I'd call my mother and say can you hear that? I knocked on
my neighbors' doors. Finally Sarah came with a doctor and
I went with them to "his office," but really it was hospital,
wasn't it, where I slept for days. I had so many dreams. And
when I woke up my mother was there, peering over me
like I was small again, and I began to cry, which I never
do . . . And she whispered "we all have our wobbles, dear,

not to worry." And when she said it, all of a sudden that was all it was, a wobble, and finally—finally it was . . . quiet.

DELILAH
. . . A wobble.
That's so British it's not even funny.

JENNIFER
Isn't it though.

(Beat)

DELILAH
And when you were in it . . . In the, um —

JENNIFER
Wobble.

DELILAH
Right. When you were in it, did you know it was happening?

JENNIFER
No. Not really. No.

*(A long beat. **Delilah** takes this in. They stare at each other.)*

JENNIFER
All right, let's open the presents.

DELILAH
But . . . it's not Christmas morning.

JENNIFER
Who cares?

(**Delilah** *is shocked.* **Jennifer** *hands* **Delilah** *a wrapped box.* **Delilah** *looks at her—she can't open the gift.*)

JENNIFER
Come on, open it.

(**Delilah** *opens the box. It's a pair of earrings. Demure.*)

JENNIFER
(*suddenly a bit shy again*)
I just saw them and thought of you. But you can always exchange them; in fact you *should* exchange them, if—

DELILAH
No, I love them. I just . . .

JENNIFER
What?

DELILAH
I didn't get you anything.

(**Jennifer** *looks at the little Christmas tree under which it seems there are more gifts than there were before.*)

JENNIFER
Then what's all of that?

(**Delilah** *doesn't know; she shakes her head.* **Jennifer** *eyes the boxes—their shapes are familiar to her. She opens one—it's her mother's jade vase. She opens another—her mother's reading glasses. Another—the elephant's tusk bookend. And then, finally—the honeypot.* **Jennifer** *begins to cry, silently. Some things DO come back. She hugs her mother's things to her. Then—the phone rings.*)

JENNIFER
Oh God that'll be the hospital.

(*It rings again. But they don't move; they're terrified. And then the lights shift.* **Delilah** *and* **Jennifer** *stand beside each other and* *address the audience—but now they hear each other and talk to us together.*)

DELILAH
In my humble opinion the ghost that haunts everyone is right in front of us.
Taunting us because we can't see it.
The future.

JENNIFER
After a little while Delilah gets on her feet again.
Nothing in this life is easy, or fast.

At the center where she stays for a bit they say they've never met someone so lucid in some respects who's also so determined she spent so much time with a ghost.

DELILAH
I meant it in a more metaphorical sense.

(*Beat*)

Probably.

JENNIFER
(*to the audience*)
And then *years* have passed. Delilah is thirty-eight—

DELILAH
Thirty-eight. Holy shit.

JENNIFER
She takes a weekend trip
to New York City
with her daughter, Deja, who's six.
They live in Baltimore. Delilah teaches Art History
so it's no surprise that today
she takes Deja to the Met.

She wants to show her how life and art have transformed
over time.
And also how they haven't.
And when they're eating lunch at the museum's crowded
café,
they call John, and his granddaughter
reports that she saw pictures *and* sculptures,
and some of the sculptures were *naked*, Grandpa,
and John will laugh,
that robust laugh that always feels like a gift.

DELILAH
At home, that night, I find the letter Jennifer wrote me
just after I left England for good when I was hoping
to put out of my mind the wobble
and the roof, and the last time I went up there,
looking for, well . . . my mother.
Of course there was nothing there. Nothing
but steam shooting skywards
that somehow maintained its shape despite the rain.
Was that my mother?
No. She was there.
And she wasn't.

JENNIFER
Dear Delilah,
I've so enjoyed our time together.
I think you're a remarkable and very strong young
woman.
To exist in this particular world
where the dams are breaking and the fires are burning.
 . . . Strength that I saw on full display
when you showed me up in step class
last week—

DELILAH
(*to the audience*)
We searched everywhere for a step class!

And finally found a deeply sketchy one in the basement of
this lady's home—

JENNIFER
Where in addition to the nice surprise of not getting
murdered,
I was astounded by your ability to . . .
keep going. I think I was pretty much spent
after ten minutes but not you.
So I just . . . watched as you pushed yourself beyond your
limits,
crashing your way through the world
like an endangered rhinoceros who knows this is it—
there is no time to waste because there *is* no time;
it's almost finished.

DELILAH
She didn't seem like someone
who could . . . disappear.
Maybe because for so long I *wanted* her to
and she didn't. Or wouldn't.
. . . But last year she did.
She died.

(Beat)

In her letter, she assured me that should I ever need her,
her door would be open.

But if it is, where is it?

The other night I took my daughter to a magic show.
At the end she was frightened and reached for my hand.
She wanted to know where the magician went when he
vanished.

I didn't know what to tell her.

When we got home it was twilight
and we could make out the soft patter of rain on the roof above us,
like footsteps.

JENNIFER
Delilah. There is a mystery all around us
and we must take pains not to puncture it.
I so rarely dream but not long after you left London
I had a particularly vivid one. I was with my mother again.
We were in her kitchen
and she was grumbling at me as usual,
full of the usual complaints,
but *now*—I couldn't take it anymore
and I yelled out: you can't do this to me!
I'm a person, just like you. A person.
And it hurts my feelings when you carp
and criticize; I'm doing my best.
Also, have you considered that maybe I want things too?!
And she looked at me and said "no, Jennifer,
I don't think I really *had* considered that."
And then she apologized to me—for what, I'm not sure,
dying maybe, or leaving me unseen
or raising me in the only way she knew how . . .

At which point . . . I forgave her. I did.
And she held me and stroked my hair—I can still feel it—
through the years, through the dream . . .
I mean, what a thing, to have a mother.

(*The lights fade to black.*)

End of play

Discover. Read. Listen. Watch.

A NEW WAY TO ENGAGE WITH PLAYS

This award-winning digital library features over 3,000 playtexts, 400 audio plays, 300 hours of video and 360 scholarly books.

Playtexts published by Methuen Drama, The Arden Shakespeare, Faber & Faber, Playwrights Canada Press, Aurora Metro Books and Nick Hern Books.

Audio Plays from L.A. Theatre Works featuring classic and modern works from the oeuvres of leading American playwrights.

Video collections including films of live performances from the RSC, The Globe and The National Theatre, as well as acting masterclasses and BBC feature films and documentaries.

FIND OUT MORE:
www.dramaonlinelibrary.com • @dramaonlinelib

Methuen Drama Modern Plays

include

Bola Agbaje
Edward Albee
Ayad Akhtar
Jean Anouilh
John Arden
Peter Barnes
Sebastian Barry
Clare Barron
Alistair Beaton
Brendan Behan
Edward Bond
William Boyd
Bertolt Brecht
Howard Brenton
Amelia Bullmore
Anthony Burgess
Leo Butler
Jim Cartwright
Lolita Chakrabarti
Caryl Churchill
Lucinda Coxon
Tim Crouch
Shelagh Delaney
Ishy Din
Claire Dowie
David Edgar
David Eldridge
Dario Fo
Michael Frayn
John Godber
James Graham
David Greig
John Guare
Lauren Gunderson
Peter Handke
David Harrower
Jonathan Harvey
Robert Holman
David Ireland
Sarah Kane

Barrie Keeffe
Jasmine Lee-Jones
Anders Lustgarten
Duncan Macmillan
David Mamet
Patrick Marber
Martin McDonagh
Arthur Miller
Alistair McDowall
Tom Murphy
Phyllis Nagy
Anthony Neilson
Peter Nichols
Ben Okri
Joe Orton
Vinay Patel
Joe Penhall
Luigi Pirandello
Stephen Poliakoff
Lucy Prebble
Peter Quilter
Mark Ravenhill
Philip Ridley
Willy Russell
Jackie Sibblies Drury
Sam Shepard
Martin Sherman
Chris Shinn
Wole Soyinka
Simon Stephens
Kae Tempest
Anne Washburn
Laura Wade
Theatre Workshop
Timberlake Wertenbaker
Roy Williams
Snoo Wilson
Frances Ya-Chu Cowhig
Benjamin Zephaniah

Methuen Drama Contemporary Dramatists

include

John Arden (two volumes)
Arden & D'Arcy
Peter Barnes (three volumes)
Sebastian Barry
Mike Bartlett
Clare Barron
Brad Birch
Dermot Bolger
Edward Bond (ten volumes)
Howard Brenton (two volumes)
Leo Butler (two volumes)
Richard Cameron
Jim Cartwright
Caryl Churchill (two volumes)
Complicite
Sarah Daniels (two volumes)
Nick Darke
David Edgar (three volumes)
David Eldridge (two volumes)
Ben Elton
Per Olov Enquist
Dario Fo (two volumes)
Michael Frayn (four volumes)
John Godber (four volumes)
Paul Godfrey
James Graham (two volumes)
David Greig
John Guare
Lee Hall (two volumes)
Katori Hall
Peter Handke
Jonathan Harvey (two volumes)
Iain Heggie
Israel Horovitz
Declan Hughes
Terry Johnson (three volumes)
Sarah Kane
Barrie Keeffe
Bernard-Marie Koltès (two volumes)
Franz Xaver Kroetz
Kwame Kwei-Armah
David Lan
Bryony Lavery
Deborah Levy
Doug Lucie

Alistair MacDowall
Sabrina Mahfouz
David Mamet (six volumes)
Patrick Marber
Martin McDonagh
Duncan McLean
David Mercer (two volumes)
Anthony Minghella (two volumes)
Rory Mullarkey
Tom Murphy (six volumes)
Phyllis Nagy
Anthony Neilson (three volumes)
Peter Nichol (two volumes)
Philip Osment
Gary Owen
Louise Page
Stewart Parker (two volumes)
Joe Penhall (two volumes)
Stephen Poliakoff (three volumes)
David Rabe (two volumes)
Mark Ravenhill (three volumes)
Christina Reid
Philip Ridley (two volumes)
Willy Russell
Eric-Emmanuel Schmitt
Ntozake Shange
Sam Shepard (two volumes)
Martin Sherman (two volumes)
Christopher Shinn (two volumes)
Joshua Sobel
Wole Soyinka (two volumes)
Simon Stephens (five volumes)
Shelagh Stephenson
David Storey (three volumes)
C. P. Taylor
Sue Townsend
Judy Upton (two volumes)
Michel Vinaver (two volumes)
Arnold Wesker (two volumes)
Peter Whelan
Michael Wilcox
Roy Williams (four volumes)
David Williamson
Snoo Wilson (two volumes)
David Wood (two volumes)
Victoria Wood

Methuen Drama Student Editions

Alan Ayckbourn *Confusions* • **Mike Bartlett** *Earthquakes in London* • **Aphra Behn** *The Rover* • **Alice Birch** *Revolt. She Said. Revolt Again* • **Edward Bond** *Lear* • *Saved* • **Bertolt Brecht** *The Caucasian Chalk Circle* • *Fear and Misery in the Third Reich* • *The Good Person of Szechwan* • *Life of Galileo* • *Mother Courage and her Children* • *The Resistible Rise of Arturo Ui* • *The Threepenny Opera* • **Jon Brittain** *Rotterdam* • **Georg Büchner** *Woyzeck* • **Anton Chekhov** *The Cherry Orchard* • *The Seagull* • *Three Sisters* • *Uncle Vanya* • **Caryl Churchill** *Serious Money* • *Top Girls* • **Shelagh Delaney** *A Taste of Honey* • **Inua Ellams** *Barber Shop Chronicles* • **Euripides** *Elektra* • *Medea* • **Dario Fo** *Accidental Death of an Anarchist* • **Michael Frayn** *Copenhagen* • **John Galsworthy** *Strife* • **Nikolai Gogol** *The Government Inspector* • **Carlo Goldoni** *A Servant to Two Masters* • **James Graham** *This House* • **Tanika Gupta** *The Empress* • **Katori Hall** *The Mountaintop* • **Lorraine Hansberry** *A Raisin in the Sun* • **Robert Holman** *Across Oka* • **Henrik Ibsen** *A Doll's House* • *Ghosts* • *Hedda Gabler* • **Sarah Kane** *4.48 Psychosis* • *Blasted* • **Charlotte Keatley** *My Mother Said I Never Should* • **Dennis Kelly** *DNA* • **Bernard Kops** *Dreams of Anne Frank* • **Federico García Lorca** *Blood Wedding* • *Doña Rosita the Spinster* (bilingual edition) • *The House of Bernarda Alba* (bilingual edition) • *Yerma* (bilingual edition) • **David Mamet** *Glengarry Glen Ross* • *Oleanna* • **Patrick Marber** *Closer* • **John Marston** *The Malcontent* • **Martin McDonagh** *The Lieutenant of Inishmore* • *The Lonesome West* • *The Beauty Queen of Leenane* • *The Cripple of Inishmaan* • **Alistair McDowall** *Pomona* • **John McGrath** *The Cheviot, the Stag and the Black, Black Oil* • **Arthur Miller** *All My Sons* • *The Crucible* • *A View from the Bridge* • *Death of a Salesman* • *The Price* • *After the Fall* • *The Last Yankee* • *A Memory of Two Mondays* • *Broken Glass* • *Incident at Vichy* • *The American Clock* • *The Ride Down Mt. Morgan* • **Joe Orton** *Loot* • **Joe Penhall** *Blue/Orange* • **Luigi Pirandello** *Six Characters in Search of an Author* • **Lucy Prebble** *Enron* • **Mark Ravenhill** *Shopping and F***ing* • **Reginald Rose** *Twelve Angry Men* • **Willy Russell** *Blood Brothers* • *Educating Rita* • **Lemn Sissay** Benjamin Zephaniah's *Refugee Boy* • **Sophocles** *Antigone* • *Oedipus the King* • **Wole Soyinka** *Death and the King's Horseman* • **Simon Stephens** *Punk Rock* • *Pornography* • **Shelagh Stephenson** *The Memory of Water* • **August Strindberg** *Miss Julie* • **J. M. Synge** *The Playboy of the Western World* • **Kae Tempest** *Wasted* • **Theatre Workshop** *Oh What a Lovely War* • **Laura Wade** *Posh* • **Frank Wedekind** *Spring Awakening* • **Timberlake Wertenbaker** *Our Country's Good* • **Arnold Wesker** *The Merchant* • **Peter Whelan** *The Accrington Pals* • **Oscar Wilde** *The Importance of Being Earnest* • **Roy Williams** *Sing Yer Heart Out for the Lads* • **Tennessee Williams** *A Streetcar Named Desire* • *The Glass Menagerie* • *Cat on a Hot Tin Roof* • *Sweet Bird of Youth*

Methuen Drama World Classics
include

Jean Anouilh (two volumes)
John Arden (two volumes)
Brendan Behan
Aphra Behn
Bertolt Brecht (eight volumes)
Georg Büchner
Mikhail Bulgakov
Pedro Calderón
Karel Čapek
Peter Nichols (two volumes)
Anton Chekhov
Noël Coward (nine volumes)
Georges Feydeau (two volumes)
Eduardo De Filippo
Max Frisch (two volumes)
John Galsworthy
Nikolai Gogol (two volumes)
Maxim Gorky (two volumes)
Harley Granville Barker
(two volumes)
Victor Hugo
Henrik Ibsen (six volumes)
Alfred Jarry
Federico García Lorca
(three volumes)
Pierre Marivaux
Mustapha Matura
David Mercer
(two volumes)
Arthur Miller (six volumes)
Molière
Pierre de Musset
Joe Orton
A. W. Pinero
Luigi Pirandello
Terence Rattigan
W. Somerset Maugham
August Strindberg
(three volumes)
J. M. Synge
Ramón del Valle-Inclán
Frank Wedekind
Oscar Wilde
Tennessee Williams

Methuen Drama
Classical Greek Dramatists

Aeschylus Plays: One
(Persians, Seven Against Thebes, Suppliants,
Prometheus Bound)

Aeschylus Plays: Two
(Oresteia: Agamemnon, Libation-Bearers, Eumenides)

Aristophanes Plays: One
(Acharnians, Knights, Peace, Lysistrata)

Aristophanes Plays: Two
(Wasps, Clouds, Birds, Festival Time, Frogs)

Aristophanes & Menander: New Comedy
(Women in Power, Wealth, The Malcontent,
The Woman from Samos)

Euripides Plays: One
(Medea, The Phoenician Women, Bacchae)

Euripides Plays: Two
(Hecuba, The Women of Troy, Iphigeneia at Aulis, Cyclops)

Euripides Plays: Three
(Alkestis, Helen, Ion)

Euripides Plays: Four
(Elektra, Orestes, Iphigeneia in Tauris)

Euripides Plays: Five
(Andromache, Herakles' Children, Herakles)

Euripides Plays: Six
(Hippolytos, Suppliants, Rhesos)

Sophocles Plays: One
(Oedipus the King, Oedipus at Colonus, Antigone)

Sophocles Plays: Two
(Ajax, Women of Trachis, Electra, Philoctetes)

For a complete listing of
Methuen Drama titles, visit:
www.bloomsbury.com/drama

Follow us on Twitter and keep up to date
with our news and publications
@MethuenDrama